Inclusive Language Guide

INCLUSIVE LANGUAGE GUIDE

An A - Z Glossary of DEIB
Terminology Relevant and
Applicable in our World Today

By **K. Clark**

Copyright © 2024 by Kirsty Clark All rights reserved. No part of this publication may be reproduced, stored in a retrieval system, or transmitted in any form or by any means, electronic, mechanical, photocopying, recording or otherwise, without the prior written permission of the copyright owner.

Although every effort was made to ensure the accuracy and completeness of information contained in this book, we assume no responsibility for errors, inaccuracies, omissions, or inconsistency herein.

First Printing 2023
ISBN 979-8-218-41055-1

Published by C.A.R.E. Culture And Relationship Experts
Printed in the United States of America
Cover Design by K.Clark
Editing and Design by K. Clark

PREFACE

"From this "Gen X'er" to my two "Gen Z'ers". I do this work for you in hopes of leaving the world and workplace better than the way I found it."

~ K. Clark

TABLE OF CONTENTS

I. Foreward

II. Glossary of Terms A - Z

III. Inclusive Phrases

IV. References

I.

Foreward

Our Language matters. And like our diverse world, the words, and terms we use as communicators continue to evolve and become more culturally competent. In this guide, you will find an A – Z Glossary of Diversity, Equity, Inclusion, and Belonging (DEIB) terminology relevant and applicable in our world today. Considering today's intersectional global work and workforce, this guide can be a useful tool for any individual or organization.

Inclusive language helps you avoid terminology or expressions that imply or are perceived to express ideas that are racist, sexist, offensive, prejudiced or otherwise biased. Being mindful of your word choice shows that you respect differences and amplifies your message to more people.

This glossary of terms is not specific to one cause or community and can edify the vocabulary of anyone who wants to speak the language of inclusion.

Using recommendations for your own purposes, teams and organizations is optional. This document is viewed as a living document and a continual work in progress. The countless hours that went into this publication were a labor of love, good faith, pure intentions and the utmost respect for all communities and individuals.

II.
Glossary of Terms
A - Z

II.

Glossary of Terms
A

A

AAPI – An acronym that stands for Asian Americans and Pacific Islanders; see API.

Able-bodied – Non-disabled, people without physical disabilities.

Ableism – Devaluing and/or limiting someone due to a disability (mental, physical, learning, etc.). Ableist language can hold bias towards the nondisabled experience or discriminate against the disabled community. For example, to be more inclusive, use "access" instead of "see" ..." experience" instead of "watch" ... "communicate" instead of "talk/hear" ... "select" instead of "click".

Aboriginal – A term that refers to an Indigenous person from anywhere in the world; more popular in Canada, but is being phased out in favor of the term; Indigenous. It also refers to a specific clan/tribe in Australia. See: First Nation and Indigenous.

Access – The elimination of discrimination and other barriers that contribute to inequitable opportunities to join and be a part of a work group, organization, or community.

Accessibility – Taking intentional steps to ensure reasonable accommodations are in place to be inclusive to employees with disabilities – i.e. being mindful of color contrast (font/background), scheduling meetings with breaks that align with your audience, embedding alternate text and graphics, adding closed captioning on videos.

Accountability – To take personal ownership and act from where you sit; the notion that all employees have a shared responsibility.

II.
Glossary of Terms
A

A

Accountability Framework – Makes roles, responsibilities, and expectations clear through a common purpose, communication, coaching and collaboration. This details an organizations commitment to drive progress by holding executive managers accountable to achieve representation goals, demonstrate inclusive leadership behaviors and use their results to determine year-end performance evaluations, compensation decisions, and organizational changes.

Acquired diversity – This term applies to diverse skills, ideas and insights gained from unique experiences. For example, working in a different country can help you gain an appreciation of a new culture, and working with diverse teammates can result in new ideas and an appreciation of different working styles.

Active Bystander – A person who steps in and speaks up when witnessing bias, microaggressions, bullying, harassment, or other harmful or inappropriate behaviors; alternatively, they also escalate their own concerns.

Active Duty – A service member who is in the military full-time, working or living on a military base and can be deployed at any time.

Affirmed Gender – An individual's true gender, as opposed to their gender assigned at birth. This term should replace terms like new gender or chosen gender, which imply that an individual chooses their gender.

II.
Glossary of Terms
A

A

African American – Typically refers to Black people in North America and does not include people of Black heritage from other locations – like Black employees in the Europe, Middle East, and Africa region. You'll generally see African American on communications that are predominately targeted for North America; see Black

Afro-Latinos (Latinas) – A term used to describe Latin Americans with mainly African roots.

Ageism – A term that describes when someone makes assumption about people based on their age.

Agender – When a person's gender identity and/or expression aligns with neither sex assigned at birth nor with any gender.

All Lives Matter – *Not Recommended.* A slogan frequently used in opposition to the Black Lives Matter movement and in today's context of the purpose and need for the Black Lives Matter movement, can be considered offensive.

Ally – A person who actively strives to create or strengthen a diverse culture of respect, equity and inclusion by advocating for or supporting different groups of people; i.e.: race, gender, ethnicity, sexual orientation, disability, social class etc.

Allyship – A lifelong process of consistently building relationships based on trust, advocating for others and creating a culture of inclusion. At its core, allyship is promoting equity and holding oneself accountable, while making an intentional effort.

II.
Glossary of Terms
A

A

American Indian – *Not recommended*. A term used to refer to an Indigenous person from the continental United States (generally used between Indigenous people when referring to each other) that is falling out of favor with some groups and being replaced with "Native American". It is also not inclusive of Native Hawaiians, Native Alaskans or Canadian "First Nation" tribe/nations.It is acceptable, however, to use the shortened term "Natives" to refer to the community instead. US Equal Employment Opportunity Commission "EEOC" reporting, different terms may be required. See: First Nation and Indigenous.

Androgynous – When a person's gender expression integrates a combination of masculine and feminine elements. For some, androgyny is about achieving a "gender neutral" expression, whereas others may wish to acknowledge their relationship to masculinity and femininity.

Antisemitism – Hostility toward or prejudice against institutions or communities and people who speak a Semitic language, i.e. Arab and Jewish communities.

AFAB – Acronym meaning Assigned Male at Birth. AFAB people may or may not identify as female some or all of the time. AFAB is a useful term for educating about issues that may happen to these bodies without connecting to womanhood or femaleness. Generally not considered an identity as calling a transgender man "AFAB", for example erases his identity as a man. Instead use a person's pronouns and self-description. See: Sex Assigned at Birth.

II.
Glossary of Terms
A

A

AMAB – Acronym meaning Assigned Female at Birth. AMAB people may or may not identify as male some or all of the time. AMAB is a useful term for educating about issues that may happen to these bodies without connecting to manhood or maleness. Generally not considered an identity as calling a transgender woman "AMAB", for example erases her identity as a woman. Instead use a person's pronouns and self-description.See: Sex Assigned at Birth.

APAC – Asia Pacific region.

API – An acronym that stands for Asian and Pacific Islanders, used to be more inclusively representative of the diaspora of the global community.

Armed Forces – The United States, Army, Navy, Marine Corps, Air Force and Coast Guard; including the reserve components thereof.

Articulate – *Not recommended* when used to compliment members of certain communities. When used to refer to select ethnic individuals, especially non-White, the remark suggests that the person in question is expected to be less competent, intelligent, or well-spoken. It can also send the not-so-subtle message that that person of a group that is not expected to have a leadership role. Instead, compliment individuals based on their ideas, insights, content, recommendations, or the information they shared.

Asexual / Aromantic (Ace) – When a person has limited sexual and/or romantic attractions.

II.
Glossary of Terms
A - B

A

Assets-based / Strengths-based language – An approach that highlights an individual's successes or achievements.

Authentic self – The complete persona of an individual, holding nothing back or keeping any part secret or tempered.

Autism Spectrum Disorder / Autism – Autism, now called Autism Spectrum Disorder (ASD), is an umbrella term used to describe a neurodevelopmental disorder and developmental disease typically diagnosed during childhood. It includes several conditions within the spectrum which changes the way someone may interact or communicate. There is no cure for Autism, but the symptoms may lessen over time. Note: Healthcare providers don't officially recognize Asperger syndrome as its own condition anymore. They used to consider Asperger and Autism as different conditions. The symptoms that were once part of an Asperger's diagnosis now fall under the Autism spectrum. Some people still use the term Asperger's syndrome to describe their condition. See: Neurodiversity.

B

BAME – *Not recommended.* An acronym for Black, Asian and Minority Ethnic, typically used in the Europe, Middle East and Africa (EMEA) region; however, it does not serve the needs of any one community and instead generalizes the experiences of the different ethnicities.Instead, it is recommended to identify the community's name directly – i.e., Black, Asian and/or Ethnic Minority.

II.
Glossary of Terms
B

B

Belonging – The notion that employees feel connected to the firm/organization and welcomed to e here as their authentic self.

Bias – A prejudice, attitude, perception, or stereotype either for or against a person, group, idea or belief that impacts understanding, actions and decisions. The preference is usually considered to be close-minded, unfair and unreasonable. Biases can be both learned and innate.

- **Affinity Bias** – A term that describes when preference is given to people who are similar to you in some way, such as race, class or shared interest.
- **Authority Bias** – A term that describes when an idea or opinion is considered more accurate or valuable because the person providing it is an authority figure.
- **Confirmation Bias** – A term that describes when you look for, remember and value information that confirms your existing beliefs, opinions and ideas.
- **Conscious or Explicit Bias** – A behavior characterized by overt negative behavior that can be expressed through physical and verbal harassment or through more subtle means, such as exclusion.
- **Gender Bias** – The tendency to give preference to one gender over another.
- **Unconscious Bias** – Social stereotypes about individuals or groups of people that are formed by a person unconsciously. Research suggests it occurs automatically as our brain makes quick judgements based on our past experiences and background. Unconscious biases are usually exhibited towards factors like class, gender, race, ethnicity and sexual orientation.

II.
Glossary of Terms
B

B

Biological Sex – *Not recommended* Instead Use: Sex Assigned at Birth. Refers to anatomical, physiological, genetic, or physical attributes that determine if a person is male, female, or intersex. These include both primary and secondary sex characteristics, including genitalia, gonads, hormone levels, hormone receptors, chromosomes, and genes. Often also referred to as "sex", "physical sex", "anatomical sex", or specifically as "sex assigned at birth". Biological sex is often conflated or interchanged with gender, which is more societal than biological, and involves personal identity factors.

Biphobia – The fear and hatred of, or discomfort with, people who love and are sexually attracted to more than one gender.

BIPOC – *Not recommended.* An acronym that stands for Black, Indigenous and People of Color. "People of Color" is thought to be an antiquated term and has a derogatory connotation. See: People of Color.

Bisexual / Biromantic (Bi) - When a person is sexually and/or romantically attracted to more than one gender.

Black – *Not recommended* to use in plural form (Blacks); instead name the community – i.e. the Black community.Black can be used as an inclusive term to encompass and refer to the entire diaspora of the Black community, regardless of their location – and is written with an uppercase "B" when referring to a person, the people or the community. You'll generally see Black on global communications that include all colleagues across the firm, as well as the external community.

II.

Glossary of Terms

B

B

Black Hat / White Hat – *Not recommended.* Use Malicious/Non-Malicious. Excludes any reference to "Six Thinking Hats" by Edward de Bono or the Black Hat Conference.

Black List / White List – *Not recommended.* Commonly used in technology to reference a list of items that are expressly not permitted, implying that all others are allowed. i.e. to list IP addresses that may not be used with a specific system; better to use "Disallow list'.

Black Lives Matter – A social and political movement dedicated to fighting racial injustice, raising awareness of police brutality against Black people and promoting racial equity.

Black Out Dates – *Not recommended.* Instead use terms like no-travel dates, bank holidays, or other appropriate terms.

Brown – *Not recommended* to refer to any group, especially the Hispanic and Latino community. It is generally considered offensive; instead use the person's ethnic community name or if applicable, use underrepresented.

Business Resource Group (BRG) – Inclusive employee groups that collaborate across regions that enable employees to share ideas, grow professionally and connect with colleagues who have similar interests. BRG priorities align to that of a firm, and all are open to every employee. These groups are different from the global DEI COEs; also known in some organizations as Employee Resource Groups (ERG) see DEI Centers of Excellence.

II.
Glossary of Terms
C

C

Cake Walk – *Not recommended*. Like "white glove treatment," this term is rooted in the history and mistreatment of enslaved African Americans in the United States; instead use; easy to do or achieve.

Caucasian – *Not recommended* to use in plural form (Caucasians) and is seen as an outdated term when referring to people who identify as White; instead use White or name of the community, i.e. the White community. The term is appropriate to use when referring to a person and those with ties to the Caucasus region, which includes Georgia, Armenia, Azerbaijan, and parts of southern Russia; however, there is some debate as to whether southern Russia is included in this region. See: White.

Chosen Name – The name a person has elected to be called; the use of a name that is different from a person's legal name.Can be a variation of a legal name or something different all together. Falling out of favor is 'preferred name' when used in the LGBTQ+ community. When a transgender or non-binary person selects a name that affirms their gender identity, that new name is usually called a chosen name. This is different for ex. when a man named "Robert" prefers to be called "Bob". See: preferred name.

Cisgender – When a person's gender identity/expression and sex assigned at birth are in alignment.

II.
Glossary of Terms
C

C

Closeted – Used as slang for the state of not publicizing one's sexual/gender identity, keeping it private, living an outwardly heterosexual/cisgender life while identifying as LGBTQ+, or not being forthcoming about one's identity. At times, being in the closet may also mean not wanting to admit one's identity to oneself.

Cissexism – A belief that there are only two genders which are assigned at birth and immutable. This prejudice has been integrated into social systems and policies, which contributes to the discrimination and oppression of transgender, non-binary, and gender expansive people.

Colored – Not recommended. This is an antiquated term; instead use the person's ethnic community name or if applicable, use underrepresented – i.e. Black, Asian.

Coming Out – The process in which a person first acknowledges, accepts and appreciates their sexual orientation or gender identity and begins to share that with others.

Commissioned Officer – (aka Officer) Generally at the highest ranks in the military, officers hold commissions and are confirmed at their ranks by their sovereign or elected government. A commissioned officer's primary function is to provide management and leadership in their area of responsibility.

Community – A group of people who share a common background or trait – i.e. cultural heritage, gender identity.

II.
Glossary of Terms
C

C

Conflict in Ukraine – *Not recommended.* War in Ukraine is the recommended way to refer to this situation.

Culture -describes a firm or organization's environment beliefs, values and how these influence policy, behavior of its employees and the way they do business. i.e. a culture where everyone is treated with respect and dignity, a culture of respect, equity and inclusion.

Cultural appropriation – When a person, group, or organization from one culture takes aspects of another culture (typically that of a marginalized community) and exploits it usually without regard to its cultural significance.

Cultural competence / Cultural Intelligence – The ability to interact and work effectively with people across multiple cultures and incorporate cultural nuances into decisions and actions.

Cultural Moment – A moment in time often based on a fixed date on the calendar (month, week, days) and sometimes tied to an ethnicity or heritage, when a firm globally recognizes a specific culture, community or group; i.e. – Black History Month, International Women's Day, Administrative Professional's Week, Holocaust Remembrance Day, Indigenous Peoples Day, National Coming Out Day. Further holidays and cultural moments can be found on a cultural moments calendar.

II.
Glossary of Terms
D

D

D&I / DEI / DEIB – Diversity & Inclusion; Diversity Equity & Inclusion; Diversity Equity Inclusion & Belonging. When companies embrace diversity of thought, experience, and ideas, but they are also more successful and attractive to job seekers.

Deadname - A term used for the former name of a transgender, nonbinary, or gender expansive person who has changed their name to affirm their gender identity.

Death March – *Not recommended*. A term used to describe projects that are taking a long time to advance. Historical contexts shows this term was used to describe a forced march of prisoners of war or other captives or deportees in which individuals are left to die along the way. Instead, refer to the projects as a slow-moving, unsustainable or impossible.

Deficits-based Language – Language that centers on what a person lacks – i.e. candidate does not have a degree.

Deployment - Refers to activities required to move military personnel and materials from a home installation to a specified destination outside of the home nation. For servicemembers and families, it has come to mean much more as deployments can vary in length and intensity. Members of the Reserve forces may be deployed and, in the US, the National Guard. When scheduled to deploy, there may be extended periods of preparation and training, resulting in a greater time commitment on behalf of the service member. Deployments are not restricted to combat; units can be deployed for other reasons such as humanitarian aid, evacuation of citizens, restoration of peace or increased security.

II.
Glossary of Terms
D

D

Disability – A broad range of physical, psychological, developmental and intellectual conditions, both visible and non-visible.

Disabled – *Not recommended.* Use person-first language when referring to an individual with a disability or people with disabilities (i.e. person who is blind vs. disabled person). Please be aware that some people see their disability as an essential part of who they are and prefer to be identified with their disability first – this is called identity-first language.

Disabled Veteran – Refers to a service member who has served on active duty in the armed forces, was honorably discharged, and has a service-connected disability or injury, or a disability or injury that was aggravated during active duty.

Discrimination – Unfair treatment because of your race, color, religion, sex (including pregnancy, gender identity, and sexual orientation), national origin, disability, age (age 40 or older), or genetic information.

Disparate impact - an adverse effect that is disproportionately experienced by individual(s) having any traits, characteristics, or status as to which discrimination is prohibited under the Constitution or any law of the United States. i.e., a pre-employment test that includes a number of questions that are not job related but have the effect of disqualifying a large number women, or men, or any other protected basis.

Diverse – Different, showing a great deal of variety, or including or involving all people from a range of different social and ethnic backgrounds and of different genders, sexual orientations, etc. *Not recommended* when used as a euphemism for non-White people.

II.
Glossary of Terms
D

D

Diverse slate – A hiring policy that requires recruiters and hiring managers to interview a diverse (different) set of qualified candidates when filling a position as a way to mitigate the potential for bias. In the U.S., a diverse slate must include at least one female applicant and a minority of any ethnicity. Outside the U.S., diverse slates must include at least one female applicant.

Diverse though / Diverse perspective – Different ideas that prevent the "group-think" mentality and generate more innovative solutions and better results.

Diversity – A term used to differentiate people in terms of what makes us unique as individuals – including, but not limited to, race, gender, sexual orientation, ethnicity, cultural heritage, disability, political, religious affiliations and more.

Diversity, Equity & Inclusion – (DEI) How a firm or organization creates and drives a holistic strategy, changing the way they incorporate a more diverse, equitable and inclusive lens into everything they do – from developing products and services, to helping communities, serving clients and uplifting employees.

Drag – A public performance that involves playing with gender norms and expectations. Performers are often referred to as drag queens and kings, whose performance and costumes often exaggerate and play with gender. Drag performance refers to expression and performance, which is different from transgender, which refers to gender identity.

II.
Glossary of Terms
E

E

Embed – To intertwine and build into the very fabric or framework.

EMEA – Europe, Middle East and Africa Region.

Empathy – The ability to put oneself 'in the shoes' of another in order to understand and identify with what they think, feel and experience. This is critical to driving a culture of respect, equity and inclusion.

Enlisted – A service member who has joined the military or "enlisted" outside of a commissioning source (i.e., Private, Airman, Seaman, etc.). Enlisted personnel are not considered a Non-Commissioned Officer (NCO) until promoted into a more senior enlisted rank where leadership responsibility significantly increases and is then given formal recognition by use of the terms NCO and petty officer.

Equality – In the workplace, equality can be defined as treating everyone the same and giving them equal access to the same opportunities. Equality may not necessarily grant equity or equal opportunity to access – and in some cases, different levels of support may be needed to provide equality.

Equity – Establishing fair treatment, equality of opportunity and fairness in access to information and resources for all. Equity and equality are not the same – equity provides what is needed to deliver equality. We believe this is only possible in an environment built on respect and dignity.

II.
Glossary of Terms
E - G

E

Ethnicity – Belonging to a social group that shares common characteristics, i.e. – language, race, cultural tradition, national heritage, religion, history, etc.

Exclusion – To leave someone or something out. Having diversity without inclusion leads to exclusion.

F

First Nation – A term that refers to Canadian Indigenous/Native American tribes/nations. See: Indigenous.

Foreign-born – Foreign-born people are those born outside of their country of residence. Foreign-born are often non-citizens, but many are naturalized citizens of the country in which they live, and others are citizens by descent, typically though a parent. See: Immigrant.

G

Gay – When a person is sexually and/or romantically attracted to the same gender. See: Lesbian.

Generational – The notion that the effect of actions can have a positive impact not only in the present, but also in the future.

Gender – Often expressed in terms of masculinity and femininity, gender is largely culturally determined and is assumed from the sex assigned at birth.

II.
Glossary of Terms
G

G

Gender Bias – The tendency to give preference to one gender over another.

Gender Binary – A system in which gender is constructed into two strict categories of male or female. Gender identity is expected to align with the sex assigned at birth and gender expressions and roles fit traditional expectations.

Gender Dysphoria – Varying in intensity, this term describes a sense of discomfort or distress when the sex assigned at birth and gender identity are not in alignment. A person may take certain measures to transition in order to alleviate this feeling. Some people who are transgender or gender expansive experience gender dysphoria but not all.

Gender Expression – How a person presents their gender identity to the world through actions, clothing, hairstyle and/or other characteristics or attributes. Remember gender expression is not equal to gender identity nor equal to sexual/romantic attraction nor equal to anatomical sex. You can not assume a person's gender identity via gender expression alone.

Gender Expansive – A person with a wider, more flexible range of gender identity and/or expression than typically associated with the binary gender system. Often used as an umbrella term when referring to people still exploring the possibilities of their gender expression and/or gender identity.

II.
Glossary of Terms
G

G

Gender-fluid – A person who does not identify with a single fixed gender or has a fluid or unfixed gender identity.

Gender Identity – A person's internal sense of their gender.

GAS / GCS / GRS / SRS – Gender Affirming Surgery is the most favorable at this time. Not recommended and considered offensive are Gender Confirmation Surgery or Gender Reassignment Surgery or Sex Reassignment Surgery (as these terms tend to emphasize a person's sex characteristics).

Gender Non-Conforming – A broad term referring to people who do not behave in a way that conforms to the traditional expectations of their gender, or whose gender expression does not fit neatly into a category. While many also identify as transgender, not all gender non-conforming people do.

Gender Queer – Acceptable when the person prefers.Umbrella term denoting or relating to a person whose gender identity does not correspond to conventional binary distinctions. See: Non-Binary as another "umbrella term".

Girlfriend / Boyfriend – Acceptable when the person prefers; "Partner" is a gender-inclusive alterative.

Glocal – An adjective in the business strategies of companies that reflects or is characterized by both local and global considerations; in a sense, to "think globally and act locally."

Good school / Good neighborhood – *Not recommended*. Instead use: Well-resourced schools / neighborhoods.

II.
Glossary of Terms
G - H

G

Grandfathered – *Not recommended.* Instead use: legacy or define terms or conditions explicitly.

H

Halo & Horns Effect – A term that describes when you perceive one great thing (or one negative thing) about a person, and it impacts your opinion of everything else about that person.

Handicapped – *Not recommended.* Use language that emphasizes the need for accessibility rather than the presence of a disability (i.e., accessible parking vs. handicapped parking).

HBCUs – Historically Black Colleges and Universities. Established prior to 1964 with the principal mission to educate Black Americans, historically Black colleges and universities are accredited by a nationally recognized accrediting agency or association. Although serving Black communities is core to their mission, HBCUs are open to all. i.e. – Morehouse College, Howard University, Spelman College.

Heritage – An inherited or established way of thinking, feeling, or doing – i.e., something transmitted by or acquired from a predecessor.

Heritage Month – A month celebrating a specific culture, ethnicity or place of origin, often based on a fixed dated on the calendar, i.e. – Black History Month, Hispanic Heritage Month, Asian & Pacific Islander Heritage Month, Native American Heritage Month. (Refer to a Cultural Moments Calendar)

II.
Glossary of Terms
H

H

Heterosexual / Heteroromantic – When a person is sexually and/or romantically attracted to a different gender. See: Straight.

Hidden Disability – Non-visible mental and physical conditions and impairments.

Hispanic – *Not recommended* to use in plural form (Hispanics); instead name the community, i.e., the Hispanic community. Hispanic describes a person from or descendent of someone who is from a Spanish-speaking country and who identifies with this term. Individuals are encouraged to Self-ID in a manner that represents their most authentic self when available. Organizations may use Hispanic and Latino to refer a person or the community. See: Hispanic and Latino, Latina/Latino, Latinx.

Hispanic and Latino – *Not recommended* to use in plural form (Hispanics, Latinos); instead name the person or community, i.e., the Hispanic and Latino communities. Recommended terminology to refer to people of the Hispanic and Latino communities. The term Latinx is *Not recommended*. See: Hispanic, Latina/Latino, Latinx.

Homeless – Person experiencing homelessness, person without housing, person in transitional housing or an emergency shelter. This term is falling out of favor. See: Unhoused.

Homophobia – The fear and hatred of or discomfort with people who are attracted to members of the same sex.

II.

Glossary of Terms
H - I

H

HSI – A Hispanic-serving institution; accredited, degree-granting, public or private nonprofit institution of higher education with 25% or more total undergraduate Hispanic or Latino full-time equivalent student enrollment.

Husband / Wife – Acceptable when the person prefers; "Partner/Souse" are gender-inclusive alternatives.

I

Illegal Alien / Illegal Immigrants – *Not recommended.* Instead use: Person who is undocumented.

Immigrant – Foreign-born individuals living outside their country of birth, regardless of their citizenship. When possible, use a specific reference to nationality (i.e., Cambodian, Canadian, Jamaican, Mexican, Pakistani, etc.). See: Foreign-born.

Indigenous American – This term, along with "American Indian" are preferred by many Native people. In the United States, "Native American" has been widely used, but is falling out of favor with some groups.

Inclusion – The creation of an environment and culture that values, celebrates and respects the differences of all employees, which allows them to contribute their perspectives and perform their best; recognizing, valuing, and fully leveraging people's differences, as well as allowing everyone to contribute their perspectives.

II.

Glossary of Terms

I

I

Inclusive growth – The firm uses this term and similar (i.e., inclusive cities) to describe our community impact work as we strive to help all communities equitably benefit, especially those that have experienced historical divestment and barriers to opportunities.

Inherent diversity – This term applies to the diverse traits that a person is born with – i.e., race, ethnicity, gender, age.

Institutional racism – This term refers to when an organization's treatment of people, policies or practices benefit one race over another. See: Racism.

Intentional inclusion – Specific, targeted actions taken to help create and strengthen our inclusive culture – i.e., participating in DEI Training, as well as small, everyday interactions with employees, clients, and customers.

Intersectionality – A theory of how one's various social identities (race, gender, sexuality, religion, etc.) intersect across different communities.

Intersex – This term refers to people who are born with genetic, hormonal, or physical sex characteristics that do not fit the typical binary notions of 'male' or 'female' bodies. There is a wide variety of difference among intersex variations, including differences in genitalia, chromosomes, gonads, internal sex organs, hormone production, hormone response, and/or secondary sex traits.

II.

Glossary of Terms
J - L

J

Juneteenth – Now a national holiday in the United States as of 2021, Juneteenth National Independence Day commemorates June 19, 1865 – the day when the last of all enslaved people in Galveston, Texas, learned that they were now free. Celebrations date as far back as 1866.

L

Ladies & Gentlemen – *Not recommended*. This is an exclusive binary greeting. Instead Use: Everyone, Distinguished Guests, Folks, You All, Ya'll.

LATAM – Latin America, Canada, and The Bahamas region.

Latina/Latino – *Not recommended* to use in plural form (Latinos/Latinas) to describe the community; instead name the community – i.e. the Latino community. A person from or descendent of someone who is from a country in Latin America and who identifies with this term. Individuals are encouraged to Self-ID in a manner that represents their most authentic self. Recommended terminology to refer to a person or the community is Hispanic and Latino. See: Hispanic, Latinx

Latinidad – A Spanish-language term that refers to the various attributes shared by Latin American people and their descendants without reducing those similarities to any single essential trait.

II.

Glossary of Terms

L

L

Latinx - *Not recommended.* An inclusive, gender-neutral and non-binary term for Hispanic and Latino people who self-identify outside of the traditional grammatical masculine/feminine suffixes of the Spanish language. Recommended terminology to refer to the community is Hispanic and Latino which represents over 22 countries. Individuals are encouraged to use the term they self-identify with and prefer. See: Hispanics & Latinos, Hispanic and Latina/Latino.

Lesbian - When a person (a woman) is sexually and/or romantically attracted to the same gender. See: Gay.

LGBTQ+ - LGBTQ+ is an inclusive term to represent the lesbian, gay, bisexual, transgender and queer community – with the plus (+) representing the limitless sexual orientations and gender identities (i.e., Intersex, Asexual/Aromantic/Agender).

Listen. Learn. Lead. – Actionable steps using a three-pronged approach to help sustain and enrich an organization's culture of respect, equity and inclusion. Aspiring and senior leaders should develop and enhance this skill and behaviors to be effective, admired, and inspiring.

o **Listen** - Strengthen understanding, help identify cultural barriers and drive inclusion to find intersections and value differences.

o **Learn** - Through every interaction, help remove bias and participate in meaningful opportunities.

o **Lead** – Take intentional actions by being an advocate for others, spotlighting behaviors that support inclusion and holding leaders accountable.

II.

Glossary of Terms

M

M

Man Hours – *Not recommended.* Instead use: Labor Hours.

Manpower – *Not recommended.* Instead use: Workforce.

Marginalized – A group of people or a community that has been treated as insignificant or poorly.

Master – *Not recommended.* The overall controlling system in an ecosystem of different interconnected systems or processes that directs the behavior of subsystem components: Better to say, "introduction controller."

Master branch – (when used together) – *Not recommended.* Instead use: Main branch.

Master / Slave or Master / Servant – (used in combination for technical communications) – Not recommended. Instead use: Primary / Secondary. Leader / Follower, Active / Standby, Primary / Replica, Writer / Reader, Coordinator / Worker, or Parent / Helper.

Masterbrand – *Not recommended.* Instead use: Corporate brand.

Mental Illness – Mental, behavioral, or emotional disorder. Specific disorders are types of mental illness and should be used whenever possible (He was diagnosed with bipolar disorder vs. He was mentally ill.) . People with mental health issues have far more sides to them than their mental illness. To accept someone as a person first is not only more respectful, but honors the many other parts to them outside of their diagnosis.

MIA / Missing in Action – Status: "Missing" is a casualty status, described by United States Code that provides for missing members of the Military Service. Excluded are personnel who are absent without-leave (AWOL), deserters, or dropped-from-the-rolls.

II.
Glossary of Terms
M

M

Microaggression – Everyday verbal, nonverbal and environmental slights, snubs, insults, actions, remarks, or questions that – whether intentional or unintentional – communicate hostile, derogatory or negative messages to a person or group based in whole or in part upon the community they align with or being to. People may even think they are giving a compliment or joking around when in fact there's a hidden insult or negative assumption underneath – i.e. telling someone their name is hard to pronounce, commenting that a person is articulate or speaks excellent English, or asking a person where they are really from.

Minority – *Not recommended.* A group of people with certain characteristics (race, religion, ethnicity, etc.) who are less in numbers than the majority group within a population. Historically, the term has been used to refer to individuals who are not White and can also have a "lesser than" connotation; however, you may still see the term frequently, as many advocacy groups, government, nonprofit and private sector programs still use it – i.e., National Minority Supplier Diversity Council, minority-owned businesses. If speaking about a group of people, population, or community, use the name of the population you're referring to – i.e., Black, Latino, Native American, women.

Mobilization – Refers to when an individual or unit in the Reserve Forces is sent somewhere within the continental U.S. or its territories. For example, a unit or individual may have been mobilized to assist with COVID response/relief efforts. Mobilizations count as deployment under the USERRA Act (Uniformed Services Employment and Reemployment Rights Act).

Misogyny – Dislike of, contempt for, or ingrained prejudice against women.

II.

Glossary of Terms
N

N

NAMR – North America region.

National Guard – Service members in the U.S. National Guard who are not full-time active-duty military personnel, although they can be deployed at any time should the need arise. They are required to attend in-person training one weekend per month and two weeks every summer. National Guardsman are the States Funded militia/military force.

Native American – A term used to refer to an indigenous person from North America. It is not inclusive of Native Hawaiians or Native Alaskans, but is inclusive of Canadian tribes/nations. In Canada, the preferred term is "First Nation", while in the United States, "American Indian" has been widely used (particularly between Indigenous people), but is falling out of favor with some groups. It is acceptable to use the shortened term "Natives" to refer to the community. See: First Nation and Indigenous.

Neopronoun – A category of neologistic English third-person personal pronouns (beyond he, she, they, one, and it). Neopronouns are preferred by some non-binary individuals who feel that they provide options to reflect their gender identity more accurately than conventional pronouns. Some examples may include: xe/xem/xyr, ze/hir/hirs, and ey/em/eir.

Neurodiversity – The concept that variations in brain functioning should not be stigmatized and that there are different ways to think and process information.

Non-binary – When a person's gender identity and/or expression aligns neither with sex assigned at birth nor within the male/female gender binary. See: Gender Queer as another "Umbrella term".Some non-binary people identify as transgender but not all.

II.
Glossary of Terms
N - O

N

A Non-binary / An agender – Not recommended. Instead use: is non-binary / is an agender person.

Non-Commissioned Officer (NCO) – An enlisted member who has risen through the ranks through promotion (i.e., Sergeant, Staff Sergeant, Petty Officer, Gunnery Sergeant, etc.) NCOs serve as the link between enlisted personnel and commissioned officers, and hold responsibility for training to execute missions. Training for NCOs includes leadership, management, specific trade related skills and combat training.

O

Officer – See Commissioned Officer.

Of Color – Not recommended. A term primarily used in North America to describe a person or group of non-White ethnicities. It encompasses not only African Americans, but all non-White groups: instead, name the specific communities.

On the spectrum – People who are considered to be within the range of a broader group, commonly used for the Autistic community, but can apply to other communities.

Outing – Exposing someone's lesbian, gay, bisexual, transgender or gender non-binary identity to others without their permission.Outing someone can have serious repercussions on employment, economic stability, personal safety or religious or family situations.

Oriental – Of, from , or characteristic of Asia. An antiquated term and is considered offensive when used to describe people. Instead name the community (i.e., Asian community).

II.
Glossary of Terms
P

P

Pansexual / Panromantic– (Pan) When a person's sexual and/or romantic attraction is not bound by gender.

People of Color – *Not recommended*. A term primarily used in North America to describe a person or group of non-White ethnicities. It encompasses not only African Americans, but all non-white groups; instead, name the specific communities.

Person-first language – Identify people first and not based on a qualified or disability – i.e. use 'person with a disability' not 'disabled person'.

Polyamorous– A term used to describe people who have the desire for multiple consenting intimate relationships at the same time. Also referred to as "ethically non-monogamous", "polya" or "polyam". There is a movement away from shortening polyamorous to "poly" since poly already means Polynesian. Consent and transparency are key components of polyamorous relationships.

Polyromantic – Refers to an individual who experiences romantic attraction towards people of more than one sex or gender, but not all. Unlike panromantic, this term implies that sex or gender is still a factor in attraction, and it does not imply the gender binary as biromantic does. See: Pansexual/Panromantic.

Poor, poverty stricken, impoverished – *Not recommended*. Instead use: Person with an income below the poverty threshold.

II.

Glossary of Terms
P

P

Poor school / Poor neighborhood – *Not recommended*. Instead use: Under-resourced schools / neighborhoods. Also *not recommended* are "bad school / bad neighborhood".

Poorly-educated – *Not recommended*. Also known as uneducated, high school / college dropout. Instead use: Person with a grade school / 10th grade education.

Pow Wow – *Not recommended* if used outside of its cultural and symbolic meaning. A pow wow is a cultural gathering still held today by many Native American and Indigenous communities.

Privilege – Advantages a person has based on specific factors – like race, education, physical ability, location, wealth.

Preferred Name - Preferred names are typically a variation of a legal name. An example of a preferred name would be when a man whose legal name is "Robert" may wish to go by "Bob". *Falling out of favor* to describe when a transgender or non-binary person selects a name that affirms their gender identity, that new name is usually called a chosen name. As a chosen name can be different from a person's legal name. See: Chosen Name.

Preferred Pronouns – *Not recommended*. Indicates that someone's gender pronouns are merely a matter of preference or something they just "like better". Pronouns, atleast for most people, are not a matter of preference but a statement of fact.

Prejudice – Preconceived opinion that is not based on reason or actual experience. There are numerous types of prejudice such as those based on someone's appearance, race, gender, disability, religious affiliation, sexual or romantic attraction, etc.

II.
Glossary of Terms
P

P

POW / Prisoner of War – Former prisoners of war are Veterans who, during active military service, were forcibly detained or interned in the line of duty by an enemy government or its agents or a hostile force.

Pronouns – Words used to refer to ourselves or other people which help prevent accidental misgendering for everyone and can be especially helpful when a name does not readily identify the gender used or for colleagues in the transgender / gender expansive community. The term 'preferred' may be acceptable when referencing names (See: Preferred Name / Chosen Name) but not with pronouns (See: Preferred Pronouns). Choosing to self-disclose your personal pronouns in your email signature line (if permitted in your organization) or on your directory page should be 100% voluntary and is one way to show support by helping to normalize their use; examples include:

o **He/Him/His** – For someone who might identify as male.

o **He/They** – For someone who might signify their connection with masculinity and alternates between pronouns.

o **She/Her/Hers** – For someone who might identify as female.

o **She/They** – For someone who might signify their connection with femininity and alternates between pronouns.

o **They/Them/Theirs** – For someone who might identify as gender-neutral or non-binary.

II.
Glossary of Terms
P - Q

P

Protected Veteran – A Veteran who is protected under the nondiscrimination and affirmative action provisions of the Vietnam Era Veteran's Readjustment Assistance Act of 1974, as amended; specifically, a Veteran who may be classified as a "disabled Veteran", "recently separated Veteran," "active-duty wartime or campaign badge Veteran," or an "Armed Forces service medal Veteran."

Proximate – Getting physically close to a person to discuss something or getting closer to a subject by discussing it with someone – i.e., being in the same room as a person as opposed to calling them on the phone.

PWD – People with Disabilities.

Q

Queer – Once considered an offensive slur. Mary parts of the LGBTQ+ community have reclaimed this term and taken back its power. Often used to provide an individual a sense of flexibility to avoid using multiple labels to describe their sexual/romantic attraction and/or gender identity and expression. Acceptable when the person prefers. Due to its varying meanings, use this term only when self-identifying or quoting an individual who self-identifies as queer.

Questioning – A term used to describe people who are in the process of exploring their sexual orientation or gender identity.

II.

Glossary of Terms
R

R

Race – The classification of people into groups based on certain physical, social, or cultural characteristics.

Racism – Prejudice, stereotyping or discrimination directed against someone of another race, ethnicity or nationality. Types of racism include individual racism, institutional racism, and systemic/structural racism. Typically, these individual beliefs, attitudes, or actions are based on the idea that people of certain races are inherently inferior to those of other races.

o **Institutional Racism** – When an organization's treatment of people, policies or practices benefit one race over another.

o **Systemic / Structural Racism** – Deep-rooted discrimination that has become ingrained in society over generations and is reflected in institutions, laws, policies and practices.

o **Colorism** – Also known as shadeism, it is a form of prejudice or discrimination in which people who are usually members of the same race are treated differently based on the social implications that come with the shade of their skin.

o **Environmental Racism** – When environmental hazards have a disproportionate impact of environmental hazards on marginalized communities. (i.e., Dakota Access Pipeline)

II.

Glossary of Terms
R

R

Redlining – A discriminatory practice that consists of systemic denial of services such as mortgages, insurance loans, or other financial services from potential customers who reside in neighborhoods classified as "hazardous" or "dangerous" to investment. These neighborhoods have significant numbers of Black, Hispanic and Latino communities and low-income residents. Redlining disregards an individual's qualifications and creditworthiness to refuse such services, solely based on the residency of those individuals in these communities.

Religion – System of faith, beliefs and practices; i.e. – Christianity, Judaism, Buddhism

Representation – Refers to the idea that if people see people like them reflected in places/roles/images, they are more likely to identify with and be able to imagine themselves as belonging as well. Representation is a good indicator of equality of opportunities and an outcome of a culture of diversity and inclusion.

Reserve – The purpose of the Reserve Forces is to provide and maintain trained units and qualified persons to be available for active duty in the armed forces when needed. The service member may be deployed along with Active-Duty personnel during times of war, in a national emergency, or as the need occurs based on threats to national security. The Reserve Forces can be called upon to serve either stateside or overseas. In general, members of the Reserve Forces are required to attend in-person training one weekend per month and two weeks per year.

II.

Glossary of Terms
R - S

R

Respect – A manner of treating people with dignity and valuing who they are, as they are.

Retaliation – Retaliation occurs when an employer (through a manager, supervisor, administrator or directly) fires an employee or takes any other type of adverse action against an employee for engaging in protected activity such as making a complaint of harassment to a governmental body or participating in workplace investigations. For example, it could be retaliation if an employer acts because of the employee's activity to: reprimand the employee or give a performance evaluation that is lower than it should be; transfer the employee to a less desirable position; withhold merit increases or bonuses, engage in verbal or physical abuse; threatening to make, or actually make reports to authorities; increase scrutiny; spread false rumors; or make the person's work more difficult (i.e. changing a work schedule to conflict with family responsibilities).

S

Scrum Master – *Not recommended.* Instead use: Agile lead designed with helping a team understand Scrum principles.

Self-ID – A voluntary, confidential and quick process that enables employees to represent their firm or organization's diversity by completing their online profile though an HR system. Aggregated data provides insights into mobility, advancement, and retention of the firm's talent, as well as informs decisions for supportive programs and initiatives.

II.

Glossary of Terms
S

S

Sex – Typically assigned to a person at birth on the basis of primary sex characteristics and/or reproductive functions. What others can't see (i.e., genetic information, physical characteristics).

Sex assigned at birth – The sex assigned to an infant at birth by a doctor or midwife based on their external anatomy and other physical characteristics. Examples are AMAB (Assigned Male at Birth) or AFAB (Assigned Female at Birth).

Sexual Orientation – A person's inherent or immutable enduring emotional, sexual and/ or romantic attraction to other people, or lack thereof, which forms part of their orientation identity. Note: an individual's sexual orientation is independent of their gender identity. See: Asexual, Bisexual, Gay, Lesbian, Heterosexual, Pansexual, Straight.

Signature Month / Week / Day – A designated time to recognize global diversity with special events that highlight intersectionality and inspire employee engagement; usually aligning to a firm's DEI strategies and are sometimes times based on the calendar, but do not have to be.

Slave – *Not recommended.* When used for Technology-related communications: One or more subservient subsystems controlled by a controlling entity in an ecosystem of different interconnected systems or processes; better to use: Instruction receiver. When used to relate to people and history, "enslaved" is recommended.

II.

Glossary of Terms
S

S

Socioeconomic status – A person's access to financial, social, cultural and human capital resources that encompasses not only income, but also educational attainment and subjective perceptions of social status and social class.

Social Construction Theory – The idea that many of the institutions, expectations, and identities that we consider natural have been created and shaped by societies and people who came before us. Things that are socially constructed still have very real influences and consequences, even if they are not based on an inherent truth. Social constructs can be reconstructed in order to better fit the society and culture they govern.

SOGI – An acronym for Sexual Orientation and Gender Identity. It is typically used as a shorthand in writing and is rarely pronounced out loud.

Spirit Animal – *Not recommended* as a slang term; it can be deemed offensive to Native American and Indigenous People. It trivializes and takes the concept of their sacred connection with, and reverence for, nature and twists it into a catchphrase and a commodity – making light of their culture and can be a damaging form of cultural appropriation.

II.

Glossary of Terms
S

s

Stealth – A term used to describe transgender or gender-expansive individuals who do not disclose their gender identity in their public o private lives (or certain aspects of their public and private lives). For example, a person might go stealth in a job interview. Increasingly considered offensive by some, s to them it implies an element of deception. Some use the phrase maintaining privacy instead, while others use both terms interchangeably. Not recommended is an alternative term: "passing" which has fallen out of favor due to its negative connotations.

Stereotype – An exaggerated or oversimplified belief about a group of people that makes a generalization or judgement about them without knowing them; based on almost any characteristic and can be positive or negative.

Stop Asian Hate – In response to racial discrimination against Asian Americans relating to the COVID-19 pandemic, Stop Asian Hate became a slogan and name for a series of demonstrations, protests and rallies against violence targeting Asians, Asian Americans, and others of Asian descent.

Straight – When a person is sexually and/or romantically attracted to a different gender. See: Heterosexual.

Strengths-based or Assets-based language – An approach that highlights an individual's successes or achievements.

Systemic / Structural Racism – Deep-rooted discrimination that has become ingrained in society over generations and is reflected in institutions, laws, policies, and practices.

II.

Glossary of Terms
T

T

Third World / Third World Country – *Not recommended.* Instead use: Developing world/countries.

Top talent – *Not recommended* if used as a qualified for any community – i.e. top Black talent, including "top" when referring to a specific group is perceived negatively, as it implies that talent in that community has to be differentiated. It is acceptable when used in relation to a firm's overall talent – i.e. As a firm, we attract and retain top talent.

Transgender / Trans – When a person's gender identity and expression does not match the sex assigned at birth. Being transgender does not imply any specific sexual orientation. Therefore, transgender people may identify as straight, gay, lesbian, bisexual, etc. Transgender people may or may not decide to alter their bodies hormonally and/or surgically to match their gender identity. See: Transition. Common acronyms and terms including female to male (or FTM), male to female (or MTF), assigned male at birth (or AMAB), assigned female at birth (or AFAB), non-binary, and gender expansive. "Trans" is often considered more inclusive than transgender because it includes transgender, transsexual, transmasc, transfem, and those who simply use the word trans.

o**Transvestite** – *Not recommended.* An older term for the word cross-dresser that is commonly considered derogatory. It was used to describe a person who wears clothes designed for the opposite sex perhaps sometimes for pleasure.

II.

Glossary of Terms
T

T

Transgender / Trans (continued)-

o**Transsexual** –A term which refers to people who consider or use medical interventions such as hormone therapy or gender-affirming surgeries or pursue medical interventions as part of the process of expressing their gender. A less frequently used – and sometimes misunderstood- term (considered by some to be outdated or possibly offensive, and others to be uniquely applicable to them). Some transsexual people do not identify as transgender and vice versa. Like the term queer, due to its varying meanings, use this term only when self-identifying or quoting an individual who self-identifies as transsexual.

o**Biologically/Genetically male/female** – *Not recommended*. See: AFAB/AMAB -Assigned Male at Birth or Assigned Female at Birth. Keep in mind however that this is not considered an identity, as calling a transgender man "AFAB", for example erases his identity as a man. Instead use a person's pronouns and self-description.

Transgendered – *Not recommended* Instead use: is trans, is transgender, is a transgender person.

II.

Glossary of Terms
T

T

Transition / Transitioning – A series of processes that some transgender people may undergo in order to live more fully as their true gender or to bring their gender expression and/or their body into alignment with their gender identity. This is a complex process that occurs over a long period of time and the exact steps involved in transition will vary from person to person. Transgender people may choose to undergo some, all, or none of these processes below:

- **Social Transition** – May include telling family, friends, coworkers, using a different name, different pronouns, changing their gender expression (i.e., starting to or no longer wearing make-up or jewelry)
- **Medical Transition** - may include hormone therapy or gender affirming surgeries.
- **Legal Transition** - may include changing legal name and gender marker on government identity documents such as driver's license, passport, Social Security record, bank accounts, etc.

Transphobia – Systemic violence against trans people, associated with attitudes such as fear, discomfort, distrust, or disdain. This word is used similarly to homophobia, xenophobia, misogyny, etc.

II.

Glossary of Terms
T - U

T

Two-Spirit – or "2 Spirit" is an umbrella term referring to various Indigenous gender identities in North America. Used to describe ceremonial and/or social roles in an Indigenous culture that would be considered LGBTQ+ in a western/colonial culture and is represented by the "2" when you see "LGBTQ2IA+", etc. It can also be used for Indigenous people who fulfill a third-gender or transgender role in society, as well as to describe sexual orientation. A person can be LGBTQ+ and Indigenous and not Two-Spirit. Note: It is never appropriate to use this term as an identifier if you are not Indigenous.

U

Ukraine – War in Ukraine is the recommended way to refer to this situation. Conflict in Ukraine is *not recommended*. "The Ukraine" is *not recommended*.

Unconscious bias – Social stereotypes about individuals or groups of people that are formed by a person unconsciously. Researchers suggest it occurs automatically as our brain makes quick judgements based on our past experiences and background. Unconscious biases are usually exhibited towards factors like class, gender, race, ethnicity and sexual orientation. See: Bias.

Underbanked – People, or organizations, who do not have sufficient access to mainstream financial services and products typically offered by retail banks and are thereby often deprived of banking services such as credit cards or loans.

II.

Glossary of Terms
U - V

U

Underrepresented – Populations that do not have proper representation – i.e., when speaking about several groups at once usually in relation to topics like workforce, social, political, and economic structures. When speaking to/about people, we recommend you refer to them by their ethnicity, if it's needed.

Underserved – A group or community whose needs are not being met or addressed equitably.

Unhoused – A term meaning having no accommodation or shelter. In recent years, this term has started to replace the term "homeless" by advocates and activists to describe individuals without a physical address. However, government agencies and research institutions continue to use the word homeless when reporting on people experiencing housing insecurity.

Uplift or Lift – Depending on the context, it may be viewed negatively when used to denote a sense of hierarchy, i.e., that a person or group is in a lower position and requires "lifting" from someone or a group in a higher position. Instead consider: equip or empower.

V

Values – Our beliefs which drive our actions.

Veteran – A person who has served in the military and has been discharged or released under conditions other than dishonorable. When referring to an individual or the community, we capitalize the V.

II.

Glossary of Terms
W

W

War in Ukraine – This is the recommended way to refer to this situation. Conflict in Ukraine is *not recommended*.

Warrant Officer – An officer appointed by warrant by the secretary of the U.S. Army, based on a sound level of technical and tactical competence. A warrant officer is a highly specialized expert and trainer, who, by gaining progressive levels of expertise and leadership, operates, maintains, administers and manages the Army's equipment, support activities or technical systems for an entire career. Warrant Officers positionally sit between Enlisted/NCO's and Commissioned Officers.

Wear Blue – A term used in relation to recognition of Autism Inclusion Month to encourage people to wear blue to show support for the Autism community; however, the term when used in relation to Autism Inclusion Month has come to have a negative connection for some people due to its association with the Autism Speaks organization.

Welfare – *Not recommended* Instead use: Temporary Assistance for Needy Families (TANF) or Supplemental Nutrition Assistance Program (SNAP) benefits.

White – *Not recommended* when used in plural form (Whites); instead name the person or community – i.e., the White community and use with upper case "W" when referring to a person or the Caucasian community – a term for people originally from Europe and adjacent regions of Africa and Asia. Specifically, this name comes from the Caucasus mountain range between Russia and Georgia. "Caucasian" is *Not recommended* and is generally seen as an outdated term. See: Caucasian

II.

Glossary of Terms
W

W

White glove treatment – *Not recommended*. Like "cake walk", this term is associated with preferential treatment, and is rooted in the history and treatment of enslaved African Americans.(Perhaps use instead, meticulous care and attention to detail.)

White List - *Not recommended*. Commonly used in technology to reference a list of items that are expressly permitted, implying that all others are disallowed. – i.e., to list IP addresses that may be used with a specific system; better to use "Allow list".

Willful Blindness – A legal term that is included in law to describe a situation in which a person seeks to avoid civil or criminal liability for a wrongful act by intentionally keeping themselves unaware of facts that could render them liable or implicated. Ex. In Banking an example would be the Bank Secrecy Act section 4.26.7.4.2 (and annual Anti-Money Laundering training) and is defined as a deliberate/intentional act to not make reasonable enquiry of potential wrongdoings. An example would be where a banker can see that their client is making suspicious transactions, but effectively ignores them so that they can keep the business. In this case, the banker could be held criminally liable for facilitating money laundering. *Not recommended* if used outside of this legal context; could be construed as ableist. See: Ableism.

II.

Glossary of Terms
X - Z

X

Xenophobia - Dislike of, contempt for, or prejudice against people from other countries.

Z

Zero sum game – The idea that if one person gains something, another person loses something. Some dominant groups may resist DEIB advancements believing that if their organization becomes more inclusive for underrepresented groups that theirs will lose power or influence.

III.
Inclusive Phrases

III.
Inclusive Phrases

Not recommended to use words outside of their cultural symbolic meaning. Ex. Let's have a "pow wow" or I've found my "tribe", and "spirit animal".

III.
Inclusive Phrases

Let's cover person first and identity first language. Here are some terms to avoid and suggested alternatives.

- Victim, survivor – person who has experienced... Person who has been impacted by...
- Wheelchair-bound – person who uses a wheelchair.
- Mentally ill – person living with a mental health condition; person with a mental disorder, person with a mental illness (name the condition).
- Abusive relationship- relationship with a person who is abusive.
- Addict – person with a substance use disorder.
- Homeless person – person who is unhoused or without a physical address.
- Prisoner/convict – person who is/has been incarcerated.
- Prostitute-person who engages in sex work.
- Slave – person who is/was enslaved.

IV. References

IV.
References

C.A.R.E.- Culture and Relationship Experts (founded by K. Clark) *is an organization that specializes in Diversity Equity Inclusion and Belonging; however, to ensure relevancy, we did hours of studying and cross-referencing from some non-affiliated yet trusted sources below.*

www.urbandictionary.com

www.dictionary.com

outandequal.org

www.allianz.com

www.hrc.org

www.eeoc.gov

Autismspectrumnews.org

www.census.gov

www.pewresearch.org

my.clevelandclinic.org

www.glaad.org

pflag.org

IV.
References, cont.

www.catalyst.org

www.psychiatry.org

www.apa.org

Wikipedia.org

www.law.cornell.edu

List some phrases that no longer feel inclusive.

Use the space below:

What is a more inclusive way of expressing the same thought?

Use the space below:

www.ingramcontent.com/pod-product-compliance
Lightning Source LLC
Chambersburg PA
CBHW060424050426
42449CB00009B/2121